Zeze
the
Copycat

Oye Akintan & Sabrina Akintan

Illustrations by Anirban Ghosh
Hardback ISBN-13: 978-1-953560-00-1
Paperback ISBN-13: 978-1-953560-01-8
eBook ISBN-13: 978-1-953560-02-5
Audiobook ISBN-13: 978-1-953560-03-2

Library of Congress Control Number: 2020944583

Oye Akintan, Sabrina Akintan, & Kids Plenty Inc.
Zeze the Copycat / Oye Akintan, Sabrina Akintan, & Kids Plenty Inc.
Meet Zeze, a five-year-old boy who annoys his sister Soso by copying everything she does. What happens when Soso gets Zeze back at his own game? Will he learn a valuable lesson, or will he continue to be a copycat?

ISBN-(hc) 13: 978-1-953560-00-1

www.KidsPlenty.com

Our Appreciation

Thank you for purchasing Zeze the Copycat. Kids Plenty Inc. would like to show our appreciation by inviting you to enjoy the free 4D Augmented Reality (AR) mobile app designed to bring this book to life. It will help children learn sight words from the story in a fun, interactive, and entertaining way.

HOW to ENJOY the FREE APP

1. Download the free **"Kids Plenty"** App to your mobile phone or tablet. (Android or IOS).
2. Follow the installation steps.
3. Read the "How to Use" section of the app.
4. Select "Zeze the Copycat" book.
5. Enjoy as the book comes to life through each page.

Do you want free coloring pages and affirmation notes?

Visit us at ***www.KidsPlenty.com***

Dedication

This book is dedicated to Xavier and Soleil.

May your light shine everywhere you go, and your confidence engulf every room you enter. Always remember, you can do anything your heart desires if you believe and work towards it.

Zeze was just five years old,
and did what all kids do.
He was a kind, happy boy,
with a strange habit, too.

When he watched TV,
at the end of the day,
he'd listen to the voices,
and repeat all they'd say.

It wasn't just the voices,
that Zeze would sit and do;
he also copied sound effects,
and even music too!

One day his sister, Soso,
tried to watch a TV show,
but Zeze copied all he heard,
which made her start to blow!

"Stop copying the TV!"
said Soso to her brother.
"My brother's so annoying—
can I swap him for another?!"

Zeze was a copycat;
he liked to tease his sister.
He poked his nose and crossed his eyes,
that cheeky little mister!

7

"Stop copying me," Soso cried,
as angry as could be.
"Stop copying me," Zeze said,
smiling, so carefree.

I have the **POWER WIT**
LEAD LIKE MLK
INVENT LIKE LONNIE J
INSPIRE LIKE BARAC
TEACH LIKE W.E.B DU

To show him how it feels,
Soso would copy too.
She'd show him it's annoying,
as he didn't have a clue.

She said, "My name is Zeze;
I'm a silly little boy.
So silly that I'm breaking,
my own favorite toy."

Zeze looked at Soso,
not knowing what to do.
His face then formed a scowl;
had she gotten him now too?!

I have the **POWER WITHIN**
LEAD LIKE MLK
INVENT LIKE LONNIE JOHN
INSPIRE LIKE BARACK O[
TEACH LIKE W.E.B DUBO[

Zeze watched as Soso laughed,
so upset at her game.
He wished that she would stop now,
doing everything the same.

Soso now showed Zeze,
how it felt to be teased.
She copied all he had to say,
which did not leave him pleased.

I have the POWER WITH
LEAD LIKE HARRIET TUBMA
INVENT LIKE DR.PATRICI
INSPIRE LIKE MICHELLE
TEACH LIKE KATHERINE

"It's not funny!" Zeze cried,
as heated as the sun.
"I don't like your teasing now,
this copying isn't fun."

I have the POWER WITHIN ME to:

LEAD LIKE HARRIET TUBMAN

INVENT LIKE DR PATRICIA E. BATH

INSPIRE LIKE MICHELLE OBAMA

TEACH LIKE KATHERINE G. JOHNSON

Zeze looked at Soso,
and pointed at his head.
"What if I don't copy you,
but Mom and Dad, instead?"

Bad idea, thought Soso.
She warned him to beware,
but Mom and Dad heard Zeze,
and told him, "Don't you dare!"

What could they mean? Zeze thought,
don't copy Mom and Dad?
Copying is a silly game,
With so much fun to be had.

29

25

A Guide to

Understanding Young Children
Who Exhibit Copycat Behavior

The Copycat Kid

When you're next faced with the challenge of dealing with a child's copying habit, and you can't figure out the how's and why's, we hope you find solace in the fact that we are all hardwired to copy. From learning to walk, to learning to talk, to smiling, and playing, everything we know was practically acquired by imitating others, and the mastery of such knowledge through repetition. Imitation is one of man's earliest forms of social interaction, and it's not going anywhere soon.

The Bright Side

When a baby giggles in response to the strange sounds you make, or blow raspberries while you make funny faces, they aren't just effortlessly melting hearts like we'd love to think. They are also bonding and developing social skills. They're observing communication through body language and facial expression and, in their little way, taking it all in. As they grow, they begin to reproduce these observed expressions in their small way, thereby mastering new skills, connecting with friends, and having new experiences, and yes, we all find it cute.

As a child begins to grow, and learning takes the forefront of their being, they'll quickly catch on. Firstly, for entertainment, by repeating everything someone says or does to tease, bother, and provoke a reaction, which often graduates into habits and character.They say imitation is the sincerest form of flattery. But in this case, kids have little to no sense of judgment, so choose to imitate without discretion or thought of the consequence for those around them.

A Child's Appropriate Copying

Before learning to guide a child's copying habits, it's essential to understand why children copy and how copying affects them. The answer, although simple, can be pretty tricky for a lot of people to accept. The fact is, copycat behavior emerges as a preschooler tool for learning and experimenting in this new environment. Imitation provides them first-hand experience with what they observe or hear and allows them to try things out.

The Preschooler's Nightmare

Preschoolers, especially before the age of three, tend to imitate a lot of what they see and hear around them. You may observe them replicating your actions and acting them out, like cleaning a work surface in the kitchen or bathing a special toy, especially when bored. They also observe their friends while at play and repeat the same actions exactly. For a child, such imitation is enjoyable, and extends to the seemingly littlest things, like spoken language.

Kids generally find mirror imitation enthralling, copying and replicating everything they see to the tiniest of details. While this is usually an excellent testament to their memory, it's also a criterion for significant social interaction and binding. Imitation also helps kids on their path to self-discovery. While at first glance, it may seem like a child copies everything, further observation will prove that they are selective in what they copy.

For instance, children tend to copy things that are out of place, like a strange sound, a funny way of speaking, or walking or dancing. They also tend to emulate people they trust, especially within their safe environment.

Since imitation is an essential emotional and learning strategy for a growing child, consider what they experience in their environment very carefully. Where possible, try to ensure that they see examples of good behavior, hear instances of appropriate language, and adopt only positive role models in their lives.

As a preschooler, the home tends to serve as this safe space. It's crucial to be intentional with what's allowed within a child's safe environment. As soon as a child begins school, the home stops being the only safe space for the child to be comfortable while learning. Home will share that role with the school environment, where they'll make friends and learn from their teachers. Through imitation, the child takes on some of the characteristics of those they copy, and naturally, you want that experience to benefit them.

Three Ways to Positively Steer A Copycats Behavior

1. **Ignore it!** Studies show that the more attention you pay to a child's behavior, even if it intends to make them stop such behavior, the more the child becomes intrigued with it. So, the key is to turn a blind eye and let the process flow. Kids will naturally shrug it off in the end and find something more amusing to focus on.

2. **Join them!** While ignoring is practical in most scenarios, sometimes you must join the child. Encourage them to copy right back in a lighthearted, funny way. You can also stop the copycat habit dead in its tracks with some tricks: You can develop a safe word for things you don't want them to do and let the child learn that word. Say the safe word and have them repeat it when they are mimicking. Doing it while they are in the act is imperative to making it effective. With time they will learn what's acceptable and what's not.

3. **Be direct.** If you observe the child copying something wrong, be direct and cut them from the source. Cutting off the source of such behavior is better than talking to the child to stop a behavior. This might include asking the source of their inappropriate copying to stop encouraging the behavior, or removing the child from the situation entirely.

Conclusion

There's an emotional aspect to imitation that we fail to realize. When a child imitates a behavior or action, especially that of a parent, it demonstrates that the child sees a role model in you and wants to be like you; this helps the child feel closer to you. In fact, imitation is often a child's way of connecting with those they love and admire, and their copycat behavior may have very positive feelings. For instance, you'll notice that they smile as they "wash" their toy dishes alongside you as you're doing the chores. So, recognize the connection the child experiences in imitating you or anyone else and join them, guide them, and help raise them into the healthiest version of themselves for the world around them.

If you enjoyed this book, please consider leaving us a review on www.Amazon.com or our website at www.KidsPlenty.com.

Our goal at Kids Plenty Inc. is to continue to create educational content that resonate with the next generation.

About the Authors

Oye & Sabrina are the parents of two amazing children who challenge them every day to be better individuals. Sabrina is a culinary enthusiast who enjoys cooking different kinds of food from all over the world. In addition to Sabrina being a master in motherhood, she holds a master's degree in Management from Cambridge College. Oye is an amateur photographer who loves taking abstract and nature themed photos. In addition to mastering fatherhood, he holds a master's in General Management with a concentration in Finance from Harvard University Extension School.

Together, they love long beach walks, music, travel, and scaring monsters away for their children. Like many parents and caregivers, they believe raising children is one of the most important jobs in the world, and they do so happily. Writing children's books and developing teaching tools to support teachable moments at different stages of learning is a passion for both authors. They are dedicated to publishing stories that empower, encourage, and help children to develop life skills in an entertaining way. Visit their website for additional learning tools at:

www.KidsPlenty.com

CPSIA information can be obtained
at www.ICGtesting.com
Printed in the USA
LVHW060306030421
683209LV00007B/686

9 781953 560001